Contents

Let there be light

Stars are like lamps in our sky. They are blazing balls made up of very hot gas. They make their own light. They make our dark sky bright.

Our sun is a star. Eight planets **orbit** around the sun. Earth is one of these eight planets. Let's learn about the sun and other stars!

orbit to travel around an object in space

First Facts

THE SUN AND STARS

by Ellen Labrecque

a Capstone company — publishers for children

Raintree is an imprint of Capstone Global Library Limited, a company incorporated in England and Wales having its registered office at 264 Banbury Road, Oxford, OX2 7DY – Registered company number: 6695582

www.raintree.co.uk
myorders@raintree.co.uk

Edited by Hank Musolf
Designed by Kyle Grenz
Media Research by Jo Miller
Production by Kathy McColley
Originated by Capstone Global Library Ltd
Printed and bound in India

978 1 4747 8684 3 (hardback)
978 1 4747 8694 2 (paperback)

British Library Cataloguing in Publication Data
A full catalogue record for this book is available from the
British Library.

Acknowledgements
We would like to thank the following for permission to reproduce photographs: ESO/T.Preibisch, 22–23; NASA, Cover; Science Source: Claus Lunau, 9; Shutterstock: Aliona Ursu, 13, Elena11, 17, isak55, 19 (Top), Kaiskynet Studio, 19 (Bottom), Roxana Bashyrova, 7, Speranto, 7 (Inset), Volodymyr Goinyk, 11, Sunti, 14, Veronika By, 15 (Insets, all), yanik88, 5, Zakharchuk, 21
Design Elements
Capstone; Shutterstock: Alex Mit, Dimonika, Kanate

Every effort has been made to contact copyright holders of material reproduced in this book. Any omissions will be rectified in subsequent printings if notice is given to the publisher.

All the internet addresses (URLs) given in this book were valid at the time of going to press. However, due to the dynamic nature of the internet, some addresses may have changed, or sites may have changed or ceased to exist since publication. While the author and publisher regret any inconvenience this may cause readers, no responsibility for any such changes can be accepted by either the author or the publisher.

FAR-OUT FACT

More than 1 million Earths could fit inside the sun.

Star light, star bright

We can see thousands of stars when we look into the night sky. There are trillions more in the **universe**.

A star is made up mostly of a gas called **hydrogen**. This gas makes **energy**. The energy turns into light that we can see. It also turns into heat that we can feel.

energy ability to do work, such as moving things or giving heat or light

hydrogen a colourless, odourless, flammable gas

universe everything that exists, including the Earth, the stars and all of space

Drawing stars

Stars are round like planets. But we draw stars with five points. Why? A bright star looks like it has lines coming out of it. These lines are rays of light. They are not really there. Our eyes just see them that way.

A star is born

A star is born in a giant cloud of dust and gas. This cloud is called a **nebula**. The dust and gas mix together. When they mix together, they heat up. This happens over millions of years. Finally a star is born!

Stars can live for millions, billions or even trillions of years. The bigger the star, the shorter it lives. The smaller the star, the longer it lives.

nebula a cloud of dust and gas

Dust begins to clump together under the pressure of its own gravity.

gravity a force that pulls objects together

The material forms a disc as it spirals inwards.

The material spirals in to the centre, forming the star.

9

The sun

Our sun is a middle-aged star. It is almost 5 billion years old. **Scientists** think it will live for 5 billion more years.

Our sun is the biggest object in our **solar system**. It is also the hottest. The sun's surface temperature is 6,090 degrees Celsius (11,000 degrees Fahrenheit). It is 80 times more sizzling than the hottest place on Earth.

scientist person who studies the world around us

solar system the sun and the eight planets and other things that travel around it

All sizes and colours

Stars come in different sizes. The sun seems gigantic. But the sun is a medium-sized star. Stars that are smaller than the sun are called dwarf stars.

FAR-OUT FACT

The stars you can see with just your eyes are much bigger than the sun. They look small because they are so far away.

Stars that are bigger than the sun are called giant stars. Giant stars are 200 times wider than the sun. Supergiant and hypergiant stars are the biggest stars of all. Some are 2,000 times wider than the sun.

Hypergiant star

Supergiant star

Sun

Giant star

Dwarf star

Stars come in different colours. A star's colour shows how hot it is. A blue star is the hottest star. It is almost 600 times hotter than the Earth. A red star is the least hot. But it is still 50 times hotter than Earth. On a clear night, you can see some of the stars' different colours using a **telescope**.

telescope tool that makes faraway things look closer than they are

Temperature of stars

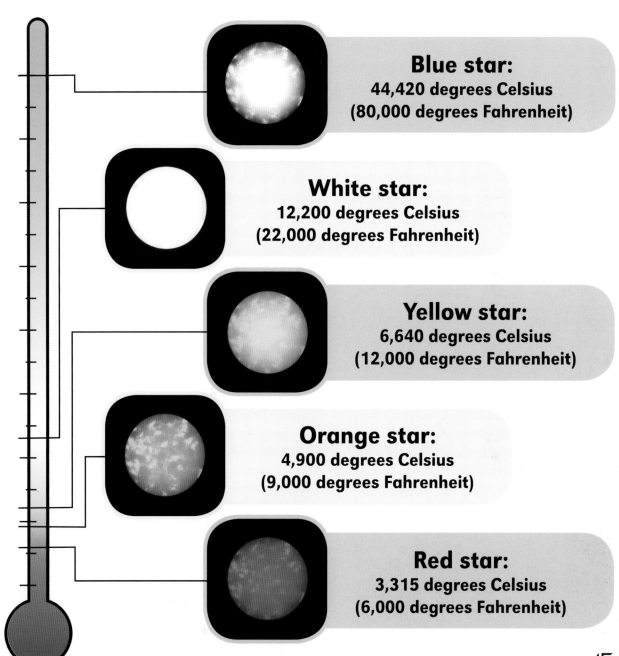

Blue star:
44,420 degrees Celsius
(80,000 degrees Fahrenheit)

White star:
12,200 degrees Celsius
(22,000 degrees Fahrenheit)

Yellow star:
6,640 degrees Celsius
(12,000 degrees Fahrenheit)

Orange star:
4,900 degrees Celsius
(9,000 degrees Fahrenheit)

Red star:
3,315 degrees Celsius
(6,000 degrees Fahrenheit)

Stars die

Stars die when they run out of gas. It is like they have run out of energy. They can't live any more. When medium or small stars die, it is peaceful. Their outer layers blow off. The layers keep spreading. Eventually, there is nothing left.

The opposite is true for big stars. If you were up in space when a big star died, it would be like watching a fireworks show. The gas from the explosion would scatter across space.

Black holes

When big stars explode, they can leave behind black holes. Black holes are like giant monsters in space. Their strong gravity pulls in anything that gets too close. They can swallow other stars and even planets. Stars and planets inside a black hole are broken apart and squashed into a tiny point.

Constellations

A group of stars is called a constellation. There are 88 constellations in the sky. By connecting the stars that look near each other, we see patterns and shapes.

Stars move through space. This means constellations change over thousands of years. We can track them while studying the sky.

Can you see why it has this name?

19

Look up!

Gaze up into the night sky. Our universe is an amazing place. You'll spot many stars. Can you spot some of the patterns the stars make? Keep studying and exploring space. What you learn will be out of this world!

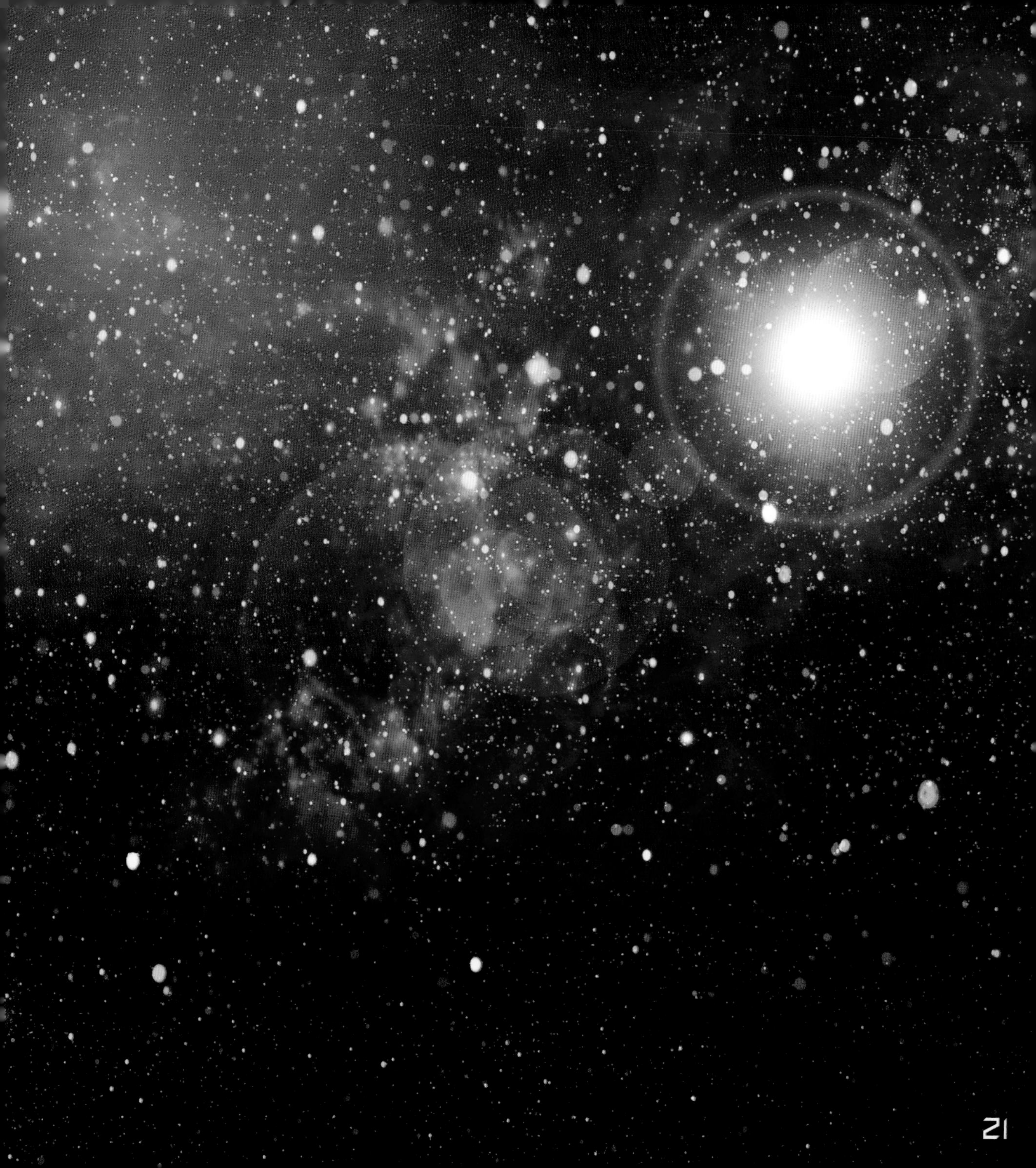

Glossary

energy the ability to do work, such as moving things or giving heat or light

gravity a force that pulls objects together

hydrogen a colourless, odourless, flammable gas

nebula a cloud of dust and gas

orbit to travel around an object in space

scientist someone who studies the world around us

solar system the sun and the eight planets and other bodies that revolve around it

telescope a tool that makes faraway things look closer than they are

universe everything that exists, including the Earth, the stars and all of space

Find out more

Big Book of Stars and Planets **(Big Books), Emily Bone (Usborne, 2016)**

First Space Encyclopedia: A First Reference Book for Children (DK, 2016)

The Sun (Super Space Science), David Hawksett (Raintree, 2019)

Websites

NASA Kids' Club
www.nasa.gov/kidsclub/index.html

National Geographic Kids
www.natgeokids.com/uk/?s=space&post_type=

Comprehension questions

- How big is our sun compared to other stars?

- What happens when a star dies?

- What is a constellation? How many are there in the sky?

Index